HAITI IS

Written by Cindy Similien-Johnson
Illustrated by Paola Velez

CSJ Media Publishing - New York

Ordering Information:
Special discounts are available for bulk purchases. For details, contact us at:
csjmediapublishing@gmail.com

This book is dedicated to
Philomène Beaubrun,
my grandmother.
Love you,
always and forever.

Haiti is

the red-orange sun and pale blue skies,

mountains beyond mountains,

emerald blue lakes and white waterfalls.

Haiti is

mountaintop castles;

and, clay houses on hilltops,

painted in sea green and turquoise blue,

coral pink and sunny yellow.

Haiti is

boys and girls in blue or pink uniforms,

children playing hide-and-seek,

the sounds of joy and laughter.

Haiti is
cathedral bells ringing;
and, churchgoers dressed in white,
singing hymns.

Haiti is

the morning wake-up calls of the rooster;

whispered secrets carried by the wind;

and, the perfect rhythm and beat of Konpa.

Haiti is

women and men at the market,

selling mangos and papayas,

fresh bread and roasted peanut candies,

griot and pikliz.

Haiti is
the hibiscus flower
Mama wears in her hair,
the strong black coffee
Papa drinks in the morning.

Haiti is
Grandpa whistling through
the gap of his front teeth,
and red dust rising
from Grandma's broom.

Haiti is

the very hot sun -

its kiss and embrace;

and, a rainstorm that starts and stops

in the blink of an eye.

Cindy Similien-Johnson is a Haitian-American Author.

She was born and raised in New York City. She studied English Literature and Creative Writing at Barnard College-Columbia University. She believes art and literature can empower men, women, and children to think courageously about the impact they can have in their own communities and the rest of the world.

Paola Velez is a Dominican-American Visual Artist.

She was born in New York, and raised in both NYC and Orlando, FL. She studied Culinary Arts at Le Cordon Bleu. She believes that art and literature can impact and change how the world views minorities.

Note from the Author

Thank you for reading this book! I always wanted to write a children's book about Haiti. The idea came to mind in December 2014 when I was asked by Ingrid Daniels (the founder of the Cornbread and Cremasse blog) to write an essay on what it means to be Haitian American. As I sat down to write, my childhood memories of visiting Haiti resurfaced. At the time, I had not visited Haiti in more than 20 years! This book is a reflection of those childhood memories.

I dedicate this book to my grandmother, Philomène Beaubrun, who passed away on May 2016, at 105 years old. After more than 20 years, I visited Haiti for the first time for her funeral. My grandmother lived a rich and fulfilled life. She was known throughout her hometown as a woman who expressed love through her actions. Her name, "Philomène," actually means "powerful love."

To continue her legacy, a portion of the proceeds from this book will go towards organizations who help rebuild the lives of people of Haitian descent. I also want to thank the illustrator, Paola. We first met at a church in midtown Manhattan in 2010. In 2016, upon hearing news of the unfair treatment of Haitians in certain parts of the world, we decided to collaborate on this project to show the world that there is beauty when Haitians and Dominicans work together in harmony for worthy causes.

-Cindy Similien-Johnson

Haiti, June 2016

41727070R00015

Made in the USA
Middletown, DE
21 March 2017